D0570893

Toucans and Other Birds

By Julie Guidone

Reading Consultant: Susan Nations, M.Ed.,
author/literacy coach/consultant in literacy development

WEEKLY READER®
PUBLISHING

Please visit our web site at **www.garethstevens.com**.
For a free catalog describing our list of high-quality books,
call 1-800-542-2595 (USA) or 1-800-387-3178 (Canada).
Our fax: 1-877-542-2596

Library of Congress Cataloging-in-Publication Data

Guidone, Julie.
     Toucans and other birds / by Julie Guidone.
         p. cm. — (Animals that live in the rain forest)
     Includes bibliographical references and index.
     ISBN-10: 1-4339-0028-9   ISBN-13: 978-1-4339-0028-0 (lib. bdg.)
     ISBN-10: 1-4339-0110-2   ISBN-13: 978-1-4339-0110-2 (softcover)
     1. Forest birds—Tropics—Juvenile literature. I. Title.
  QL695.5.G85 2009
  598.7'2—dc22   2008032240

This edition first published in 2009 by
Weekly Reader® Books
An Imprint of Gareth Stevens Publishing
1 Reader's Digest Road
Pleasantville, NY 10570-7000 USA

Copyright © 2009 by Gareth Stevens, Inc.

Executive Managing Editor: Lisa M. Herrington
Senior Editor: Barbara Bakowski
Creative Director: Lisa Donovan
Designers: Michelle Castro, Alexandria Davis
Photo Researcher: Diane Laska-Swanke
Publisher: Keith Garton

Photo Credits: Cover © Shutterstock; pp. 1, 9, 11 © Staffan Widstrand/naturepl.com; p. 5 © Justine Evans/naturepl.com; p. 7 © Nick Gordon/naturepl.com; p. 13 © Thomas Marent/Minden Pictures; p. 15 © Theo Allofs/Visuals Unlimited, Inc.; p. 17 © David Tipling/naturepl.com; p. 19 © Pete Oxford/ Minden Pictures; p. 21 © Edward Parker/Alamy

Printed in the United States of America

1 2 3 4 5 6 7 8 9 10 09 08

Table of Contents

Boldface words appear in the glossary.

Tree Houses

Toucans and many other birds live in **rain forests**. Rain forests are warm, wet places with tall trees and other plants.

toucan

Most rain forest birds make their homes in high treetops. There, they stay safe from enemies on the ground. They also find food, such as fruits and seeds.

seeds

Bright-Colored Birds

Many rain forest birds have bright, beautiful colors. The toucan is known for its large, colorful **bill**, or beak.

bill

The long bill helps a toucan reach fruits and berries on branches. Toucans also catch and eat insects and frogs.

The scarlet macaw (muh-KAW) is a big parrot. It has a bright red head with yellow and blue or green on its strong wings.

scarlet macaw

Scarlet macaws live at the top of the tallest trees. They squawk loudly as they fly in pairs or small groups.

Huge Hunter

The harpy eagle is one of the largest and strongest eagles. It has a double **crest**, or bunch of long feathers, on its head.

crest

harpy eagle

17

Harpy eagles build a big nest of sticks high in a tree. There, the eagles feed their baby, called a **chick**. Harpy eagles hunt animals such as monkeys, snakes, and lizards.

adult

chick

Birds in Danger

Toucans, scarlet macaws, and harpy eagles are **endangered**. They lose their homes when rain forest trees are cut down. People are working to protect the rain forests.

Glossary

bill: the beak of a bird

chick: a baby bird

crest: a bunch of long feathers on the head of a bird

endangered: in danger of dying out completely

rain forests: warm, rainy woodlands with many types of plants and animals

For More Information

Books

Harpy Eagles. Animals of the Rain Forest (series). Sandra Donovan (Raintree, 2002)

Toucans. New Nature Books (series). Mary Ann McDonald (Child's World, 2006)

Web Sites

Mongabay Kids: Rain Forest Birds
kids.mongabay.com/elementary/203.html
Watch a slide show of rain forest birds.

Passport to Knowledge: Passport to the Rain Forest
passporttoknowledge.com/rainforest/main.html
Make a virtual visit to the rain forest. Click on "Ecosystem" to learn more about toucans, scarlet macaws, and harpy eagles.

Index

About the Author

Julie Guidone has taught kindergarten and first and second grades in Madison, Connecticut, and Fayetteville, New York. She loves to take her students on field trips to the zoo to learn about all kinds of animals! She lives in Syracuse, New York, with her husband, Chris, and her son, Anthony.